REAL LIFE ON A BUDGET:

17 Practical Challenges to Live and Thrive on a Budget

JESSI FEARON

WWW.THEBUDGETMAMA.COM

COPYRIGHT

Published by Jessi Fearon at Amazon

© 2015 by Jessi Fearon

All rights reserved. No part of this publication may be reproduced, distributed, stored in a retrieval system, or transmitted in any form or by any means, including photocopying, recording, or other electronic or mechanical methods, without the prior written permission of the publisher, except in the case of brief quotations embodied in critical reviews and certain other noncommercial uses permitted by copyright law.

The information in this book is heavily based on personal experience and anecdotal evidence. Although the author has made every reasonable attempt to achieve complete accuracy of the content in this book, they assume no responsibility for errors or omissions. This information is to be used at your own risk.

Every situation is different and will not be an exact replica of the examples given in this book. The author cannot guarantee results or any specific outcomes gleaned from using the methods outlined in the following pages.

The websites recommended in this book are intended as resources for the reader; the author cannot guarantee their content for the life of this book.

TABLE OF CONTENTS

Before We Begin	*Page 7*
The Most Important Question to Ask	*Page 9*
Setting Financial Goals	*Page 13*
Make a Basic Budget	*Page 21*
Helpful Money Saving Ideas	*Page 31*
Identify Budget Wreckers	*Page 37*
Ditch the Spending Habit	*Page 45*
The Spender vs. The Saver	*Page 51*
Stop Living Paycheck to Paycheck	*Page 57*
Build an Emergency Fund	*Page 63*
Dump the Debt	*Page 67*
Develop a Positive Cash Flow	*Page 73*
Breaking Bad Money Habits	*Page 79*
Don't be Cheap	*Page 85*
Money Minute	*Page 91*
Get a Handle on Unexpected Expenses	*Page 97*
Don't Burden Your Loved Ones	*Page 103*
Apply the 50/20/30 Framework	*Page 109*
Stick to It	*Page 115*
About the Author	*Page 119*
Acknowledgements	*Page 121*
Resources	*Page 123*

BEFORE WE BEGIN…

Once upon a time, I was struggling to afford my life. Not because I was homeless or had no job, but because I was horrible with money. All around me, my friends were living the "good life" with all their nice, fancy stuff. I wanted that life – the Coach purse, the amazing pair of high heels that would make me look more professional, the gorgeous comforter that promised to help me sleep better at night. Those were just some of the silly things I wanted—that I claimed to need—when I was spending more money than I was making. I was more than a shopaholic; I treated money like something I was entitled to instead of treating it like a tool and making it work for me.

What made it worse is that my mom is one of the most frugal people you could ever meet. Growing up she taught me everything about living a great life with less. However, being a trueborn rebel at heart, I refused to put into practice anything my mom had taught me. When I finally hit rock bottom, I was drowning in a sea of consumer debt and faced with the harsh reality of my poor decision-making. Thankfully, I let go of my pride and put into practice all those lessons in frugality that my mom had attempted to teach me as a child. Since many people are not blessed with a thrifty mom like mine, I started my blog, *The Budget Mama*, to help those who are struggling to find balance with their money. *The Budget Mama* is where I share my family's *real life on a budget* in all its gory details.

This book is a compilation of the different ways that I have found to live a *real life on a budget*.

Living a *real life on a budget* isn't as complicated as you might think. Budgeting is not some mystical apparatus that only people in books use. Budgeting is a tool that real people can, and do, use in their everyday lives. The "B" word gets a bad rap in our society because it is viewed as restrictive. We tend to think of budgets as prison sentences for our lives, instead of viewing them as road maps for our money.

This book will inspire you to build, maintain, and thrive on a budget. It will provide you with the necessary tools to get you living your own *real life on a budget*. You just have to supply the manpower behind these tools.

Best of luck in your budgeting adventures!

XoXo,

Jessi

THE MOST IMPORTANT QUESTION TO ASK

"Money, like emotions, is something you must control to keep your life on the right track."

Natasha Munson

One of the most fundamental questions that you must ask yourself before setting a budget, determining your financial goals, or even paying off debt is this: "Why is money important to me?" You would not expect a doctor to prescribe you something without first asking you to describe what is wrong. In the same way, you should not expect to figure out how to best make your money work for you without first knowing why it is that money is important to you.

Why is money important to you?

Now, it may be tempting to just throw up an answer like "freedom" or "peace of mind," but those answers will not help you figure out a financial plan for your future. They are too vague. We need something more concrete, more in depth.

Questions to Ask to Get You Thinking

Keeping in mind that we are looking for specifics, answer the following questions to help you determine why money is important in your life.

-Why do I invest so much of my money and time on X?

-Why do I spend so little on Y when I claim it is so important?

-Why do I save as much (or as little) as I do? What am I hoping to achieve?

"The calendar and the checkbook never lie."

The truth is most of us want more time with our loved ones or more time to travel and do the things that we truly love. The problem is that we spend money in a way that is actually preventing us from enjoying our lives.

We claim that our families are most important, but we fail to save any money to protect them in an emergency. We claim that our education is most important to us, but we fail to put any money aside to actually go to school. We claim that becoming debt-free will allow us more freedom, but then we fail to do anything to help us become debt-free.

This is why you should ask yourself why money is important to you-- so you can sit down and dig deep. We make many claims about why money is important to us but fail to do anything about it. The truth is, if these things were that important we would actually do something about them.

Why is money important to you? This is a question that we all should ask before developing our financial plan. After all, if we don't know why money matters to us, how can we plan to use it?

Challenge 1: Why Is Money Important to You?

Dig deep, real deep, and ask yourself why money is important to you. This is critical to understanding not only your own individual financial needs, but also to understanding your family's needs. If you are married, I suggest that you and your spouse answer this question individually. Then discuss your answers and how to best tailor them to help your family.

Do not get hung up on "well this is only important to me right now but this will change in a few years." Life happens and your views on money will change. That is why is it important for you to revisit the question often and to make sure that you are still using money in a way that is in line with your goals.

FINANCIAL GOALS

"If we don't take the time to put our long-term goals first, there will never be enough time or energy for our dreams."

Ruth Soukup, founder of LivingWellSpendingLess.com

If you aren't setting financial goals, you are letting your money control you instead of controlling your money.

I am sure if you have ever read a time management book, you have probably read the story about the professor and the jar of rocks. In case you have no idea what story I am referring to, I will paraphrase it for you:

> A professor held up a jar of rocks in front of his class. He asked them, *"Is this jar full?"* They all agreed that it was in fact full. Then he took a bag of small pebbles and poured it into the jar. The pebbles filled in the space around the jar and he asked, *"Now is it full?"* Everyone again said yes. He then took a bag of sand and poured it into the jar. The sand filtered through the rocks and pebbles until all the space was filled. *"What about now?"* he asked, *"Do you think it is full?"* For the third time the class said yes. Finally, he took a pitcher of water, poured the water into the jar until it was all the way to the brim, and began spilling over the top. *"Now,"* he said, *"we can say the jar is really full."* He then explained, "Had I started with the water first, then the sand, then the pebbles, there'd be no room for the rocks."

The moral of this story is that if you take care of the big stuff first, you will have more time for the smaller (and possibly more important stuff) later. Thus, if you take care of the big financial goals first—emergency savings, paying off debt, or saving for retirement— there will be more money and time for the enjoyable stuff like vacations.

Setting realistic goals is the key to figuring out how you need to budget your money and where you ultimately want your money to take you. Without realistic goals in place, you will ultimately become overwhelmed and will opt for doing nothing instead of taking action to improve your financial situation. Remember money is a tool – use it effectively; do not let it use you. These three steps will help you set realistic financial goals:

Step One: List Your Priorities

Only you know what is important to you and your family. Is it paying off credit card debt? Saving for a house? Building up an emergency fund? Whatever is important in this season of your life is where you need to start. Take a moment to write down what your number one priority is for your finances. Writing it down and posting it where you and your family can see it is essential to making the goal happen.

Now, you may be saying: "We want to pay off debt, build up an emergency fund, *and* save for a house. So, where do *we* start?"

Pick only one goal to work toward at a time – remember the jar of rocks story. Picking one at a time will help you realize your other goals. If you don't have an emergency fund saved up, start there and then move on to paying off debt or saving for retirement.

Step Two: Set Specific Goals

"You must have long term goals to keep you from being frustrated by short term failures." Charles C. Noble

Give yourself specific deadlines to complete your goals. For instance, my husband and I set a pretty ambitious goal of paying off my student loans by December 2015. Is there a possibility that this may not happen? Absolutely! But the point is that by giving ourselves a deadline, we are more apt to try to make that deadline. This is what is considered a long-term goal: something that is in the future but not necessary twenty years from now.

Next to where you wrote your number one financial priority, write down a deadline for that goal. Be realistic enough to know that it may take a year or more to meet that goal. For example, last year when we decided to pay off my student loans, we knew that there was no way we could realistically meet that goal by that December (2014). But it is very possible that we could meet our goal in December 2015 if we stick to our plan. Make sure your deadline is realistic.

Now that your long-term goal is written down with a realistic deadline, set some short-term goals. Think of these as the "pebbles" in the jar of rocks story; they are smaller pieces to your long-term goal that can be attained in thirty to sixty days.

For example, if your long-term goal is to save $2,000 in an emergency fund, you can start by contributing 2% of every paycheck towards your emergency fund for the next thirty days. Afterwards, you can bump it up to 4% of every paycheck and continue this trend every thirty days until you realize your goal of $2,000.

Step Three: Eat the Frog

Mark Twain is often quoted, "If you eat a live frog for breakfast, chances are that will be the worst thing you have to do all day." Mr. Twain's point is that if you tackle the hardest, least enjoyable task first thing in the morning, and do not accomplish much else during the day, you will still have accomplished a lot.

In terms of your financial goals, make a point to meet your short-term goals first—even if the very idea of that goal is painful. If you've decided to contribute 2% towards your emergency fund, or that you will submit a more-than-the-principal payment on your car loan each month, make sure you meet that goal before you spend money on anything else. Completing your "eat the frog" tasks as soon as possible each month (after you have paid other bills but before you spend any other money) will make realizing your goals easier. Whatever it may be that you need to accomplish today in order to realize your long-term goal in the future, get it done now. Don't wait for tomorrow.

Challenge 2: Set S.M.A.R.T. Goals

Take some time this week to create long-term and short-term goals for your family's financial well-being. If you are married or share money with someone else, it is essential that you work alongside that person when creating these goals. You both have to work together towards your goals or else you will never realize them.

When you sit down to create your goals, use the SMART method to generate realistic financial goals. SMART stands for specific, measureable, achievable, realistic, and timely.

Let's look at how my family's goal of paying off my student loan by December 2015 is a SMART goal:

It is *specific* because we know the exact dollar amount that we are trying to pay off and when we'd like to accomplish this goal.

It is *measureable* because we know how much extra we need to pay on my loans in order to achieve our goal. Every month we can ask ourselves, "Did we meet our goal this month?"

It is *achievable* - it would not have been achievable in 2014 but it is in 2015.

It is *realistic* since it is something that can be done.

It is *timely* because there is a set deadline to meet, but it also fits in where we are currently in our debt payoff plan. We paid off all our credit cards in 2013 and decided to get rid of our expensive car loan and purchase an older used vehicle in 2014. Therefore, we only have two debts left to pay – my student loans and our mortgage. It would not make sense to attempt to pay off my loans first if we still had high interest credit card debt.

When I consider this goal, I feel confident that we will be able to do exactly what we've set out to do. My husband and I sat down together, looked at our monthly budget, and decided on a dollar amount and a time line that we knew would be reasonable. I want to encourage you to evaluate the long and short term goals you've written down by the SMART standards. As long as you set SMART goals, you will get results!

MAKE A BASIC BUDGET

"Financial success is more about behavior than it is about skill"

Carl Richards, *The One-Page Financial Page*

If you are going to live a real life on a budget, you need a budget. There are only four basic steps to setting up a budget; the difficult part is actually sticking to it. Remember to exercise self-discipline in order to stick to your budget.

Step One: Determine Your Monthly Income

The first step is to gather up your paycheck stubs (or look at your past month's bank statement of deposits). If you are paid the same amount each pay period, your income is easier to determine. Just add up the totals from the past month after any taxes. Make sure that when you are determining your income for the next month you count how many paydays you will have that month. Some months have more paydays than others do.

If you have an irregular income, you will have to come up with an average amount that you expect to be paid each month. Work backwards by first figuring out what your expenses are for the month (step two) and then determine what your income must be for the month in order to break even. Keep detailed records and always record the time you've spent working with clients (this will help you determine if you are charging enough for your services). Keeping detailed records will make the budgeting process easier if you have an irregular income.

Step Two: Determine Your Monthly Expenses

Start with the easy expenses to determine: the monthly ones. Gather up all your regular monthly bills (utilities, insurance, car payments, etc); try to have the statements from the last three months for all non-fixed payment accounts (typically, this will be your utilities). Once you have your statements, write out by hand how much each one is. For the utilities, you will need to come up with an average based on the last three months. You do this is by adding up the total amount due on each bill and then dividing by three. Round up whatever number you get and use this number as your expected monthly amount for that utility bill.

Once you are finished with determining your regular monthly expenses you should have something that looks similar to this:

>Car Payment: $400
>
>Insurance: $100
>
>Mortgage/Rent: $800
>
>Water: $30
>
>Power: $80
>
>Gas: $25
>
>Phone(s): $75
>
>Internet: $60
>
>Cable: $50
>
>Loans: $300
>
>Savings: $100

Tip: Round all your expense numbers **up** and round all your income numbers **down** when making a budget - this will make doing the math easier.

Now that you have determined your monthly expenses, you can move on to the more challenging expenses: the day-to-day ones. The best way to do this is to look at your previous month's bank statement. When looking at your bank statement, cross out anything that does not apply (like the monthly expenses you calculated above, or your income). Once you can actually see what your expenses are, start going through them with a fine-tooth comb.

Start by trying to determine which ones are grocery-related, as that is typically the next biggest expense after utilities. Once you determine how much you spent on groceries last month, determine how much you spent on fuel/transportation. As you find these transactions, cross them off in order to better keep up with what you have calculated and have not calculated. After you have your grocery and fuel expenses determined look through the remaining expenses. What were these expenses? Clothing? Haircuts? Do not remember?

If you know what the remaining transactions were for, then you can determine a budget category (i.e. car maintenance, clothing, entertainment, etc.) for that expense and write down the expense amount. If you do not know what the purchases were for then they are incidentals. In other words, these are the first expenses that you will want to try to cut back on in step three.

Now you should have something that looks similar to this on paper:

>Car Payment: $400
>
>Insurance: $100
>
>Mortgage/Rent: $800
>
>Water: $30
>
>Power: $80
>
>Gas: $25
>
>Phone(s): $75
>
>Internet: $60

Cable: $50

Loans: $300

Savings: $100

Groceries: $400

Fuel: $250

Clothing: $100

Incidentals/Misc.: $150

You can now take your monthly income and subtract it from your expenses to determine if you are in the red or not. "The red" means that you have a negative balance when you subtract your income from your expenses. Do not panic if you are in the red, many people are. Moreover, even if you live and breathe by a budget it is always possible to get back in the red. Having a budget means you have a plan for your money and will make getting out of the red easier.

Step Three: Determine Where You Can Squeeze

This may be a challenging (but very doable) step. This step requires that you take a very hard and honest look at the expenses you configured in step two. If you are very deep in the red, you are going to have to really focus and cut back on as much as you can. If you are hanging on by a thread, you may also want to buckle down and figure out ways to cut some expenses out.

There are several ways to cut back, some easier than others. The first big budget buster is incidentals. If you are spending money on things that you do not necessarily need right now you may want to halt your spending. In other words, if you are frequently going to Target and you find yourself walking out with about five other items that you did not intend on buying, then you really need to stop shopping at Target for a while.

It is very easy to justify all those little purchases. The "oh it's just a dollar" or "wow, that's an awesome sale price" buys. When you cut yourself off, you will see the big picture of how much you are spending where you do not need to be.

Another place to cut back is on entertainment. Entertainment is often classified as "fun money." I am not implying that you cannot have fun but if you are in the red, you need to consider *free* fun. Trust me; kids can make their own fun and so can adults. Pinterest has a plethora of ideas for free and frugal fun.

Another entertainment cost that can really drain a budget is cable/satellite. You really may want to consider letting go of cable T.V. for a while. In addition, your cell phone(s) can really bust a budget. Consider how much you are paying each month and think about cutting your data and text messaging off for a while. If you have the internet and a computer, do you really have to have it on your phone too?

There are also ways to save on your regular monthly expenses. Start searching and gathering quotes from other insurance and utility companies. You might be surprised at how much money you can save by being willing to switch. Call your utility providers and see what options they have as far as rates go. I know I have saved us just over a $100 by fixing our gas utility bill's rate. You may be able to do the same - or switch providers if possible.

Another place we spend a lot of money on is convenience. Consider allowing yourself to be inconvenienced in order to save money. Start making your own cleaners, cooking meals at home, using cash instead of debit, using coupons, using refillable containers, etc. The next chapter will give you more ideas on areas that you can slash your budget by being inconvenienced.

Step Four: Set Up Your Budget

You will set up your budget using the information you gathered in steps 1-3. There is no right or wrong way to set up your budget. In fact, you may go through many formats before you find one that works best for you.

I prefer to write out my budget by hand, as I have found that helps me keep better track. However, I know that is not how everyone likes to do it. If you prefer a more computerized approach (where you can set up email reminders, etc.) I suggest you try a free site like Mint.com or LearnVest.com. There are even paid services such as YouNeedaBudget.com that can help you set up a budget and give you helpful insights to how your money is moving around every month. There are also several apps that you can use; my favorites are Dave Ramsey's EveryDollar and a new savings service called Digit (you can sign up here to start saving today: https://digit.co/r/WkOch?wp).

Regardless of how you decide to maintain and set up your budget, the basic way that your budget should function is as follows:

Total Income – Total Monthly Expected Expenses = Difference to be applied towards savings/Debt payoff

You will need to track your actual expenses and apply the same formula above.

Total Actual Income – Total Monthly Actual Expenses = Difference to be applied towards savings/Debt payoff

This basic budget is the budget that I made when I was financially struggling. I like to tell others that this budget saved my life because it forced me to take ownership of my mistakes. It forced me to take responsibility for how I manage my money. I believe that even the simplest budget can improve anyone's financial life.

When I made this basic budget, I was 21 years old and about to be evicted from my apartment. I had over $11,000 of credit card debt alone and a brand new car. I was living a life well above my pay grade. I was an administrative assistant making an annual salary of $18,500. I was struggling to feed myself and to buy dog food for my eighty-pound Boxer.

This basic budget was the first step to digging me out of financial trouble and to creating the life I have always wanted to live. Take this scary first step by completing challenge number three and start taking ownership of your money.

Challenge 3: Build a Basic Budget

Before you can gain control over your money, you have to develop your plan. Build a basic budget using the four steps listed above and make a commitment to sticking to your budget. It takes time to craft a well-developed budget and make sticking to it a habit. Give yourself grace and remember to stick with it even when it feels impossible. You will feel better about how your money works when you have a written budget.

If you need a printable budget to go by, you can go to http://thebudgetmama.com/2014/12/beginners-guide-budgeting.html for a free Beginner's Guide to a Monthly Budget Worksheet printable.

HELPFUL MONEY SAVING IDEAS

"I'd like to live as a poor man with lots of money."

Pablo Picasso

Saving money is a challenge with numerous ways to make it work. The biggest issue with saving money is that most of us believe that saving money is only linked to couponing, sales, and ways to stretch your clothing budget further or earning free money.

However, there is another potential way that you could save even more money. By stepping out of your comfort zone and inconveniencing yourself a little, you can save $100s over the course of a year. These suggestions may seem cumbersome at first, but they will pay off in the end!

Paper Towels

Get rid of them and replace with white bar-mop style kitchen towels. You can save an average of $260 a year by making the switch. You can purchase bar-mop cloths anywhere and buying them in white allows you to bleach any stains. Bar-mop cloths are super absorbent and can be reused multiple times. Keep them next to your kitchen sink in a pretty container and you are all set! (I admit that this one annoys all my neighbors when they come over and it annoyed my hubs for a long time too, until he realized it truly does save us money.)

Detergent

Make your own homemade laundry detergent. Making your own detergent can seem time consuming but it will save you a ton over the course of the year. Most homemade laundry detergent recipes will cost you roughly $0.06 a load to make; my family has saved over a $1,000 in eighteen months just by making our own laundry detergent. Another way to save in the laundry room is to line dry your clothing. (This is great to do with little ones' clothing – they dry fast hanging up.)

Daily Shower Cleaner

You can make this at home, too! All you need are equal parts vinegar and water. To cover up that vinegar smell you could use lemon or orange juice. If you have any essential oils at your disposal, you could add a drop or two to the solution. Possible savings: $20 a year (per bathroom)

Fabric Softener

Use ¼ cup of vinegar in your washer's fabric softener compartment and you could save an average of $78 a year. (I promise, it will NOT make your clothes smell like a pickle factory.)

All Purpose Cleaner

Use a more concentrated version that requires you to dilute before use. This can be a little more expensive up front, but since you will not need to purchase it as often you could potentially save over $70 a year. Another option for an all-purpose cleaner is equal parts water and vinegar.

Refill Liquid Hand Soap Dispensers

Instead of spending a bundle every couple of weeks replacing your hand soap dispensers, consider buying a large liquid hand soap container and refilling all of your already-purchased hand soap dispensers. Possible savings: $100 a year. If you are worried about germs, you can purchase a dishwasher safe refillable liquid hand soap dispenser and run it through the hottest cycle before refilling.

Floor Cleaner

Use ½ cup vinegar for every gallon of water. This solution does not leave a sticky residue and is safe for hardwoods, laminate, and tile. If you have a spray mop that does not have a refillable charger, just poke a hole at the top of the charger and use a funnel to refill as many times as needed. If your spray mop does not come with a washable/re-useable cloth, just use a microfiber cloth instead of the disposable ones. Possible savings: $75 a year.

If you decide to use all of these options, you could possibly save your family an average of $600 a year. It may be a little more work than you're used to, but considering the time that it would take you to clip the coupons, search the sales, get in your car, drive to the store(s), and back home, you could have made every item on this list yourself and saved the trip (and the gas!).

I personally use all of these methods of being inconvenienced to save our family money and now, they no longer seem so inconvenient.

Bonus Challenge: Be Inconvenienced

Allow yourself to be inconvenienced! Look over the budget you made and pick at least one item that you could slash from your budget in exchange for a more "inconvenient" option. It will not be easy, but sometimes the hardest changes are the most worthwhile ones.

IDENTIFY BUDGET WRECKERS

"A simple fact about success is that it requires a lot of positive, personal motivation to achieve."

Zig Ziglar, Author of *Born to Win*

Even after you create your basic budget, you may have issues sticking to your well-crafted budget. Budgeting is tough, but it is the first step towards taking responsibility for your money.

If your budget has not been working, it could mean serious financial trouble for you or your family later down the road. I know that you do not want that and neither do I. Therefore, I am going to share with you seven reasons why your budget may not be working and what you can do to fix it.

1. Allocating Too Much Money towards One Expense and Not Enough towards Another

Let us say, for example, you budgeted a huge amount for paying off debt this month but little to no money towards clothing. Normally, that may be fine, however, your kids start school this month and they need new clothes for the school year.

You just wrecked your budget because you forgot to account for a major expense – your kids' back-to-school wardrobe.

Solution: Make a list of all the expected expenses for the month *before* making your budget in order to ensure that you are accounting for all the necessary expenses.

2. Outside Influences

I am not just talking about people influencing you to wreck your budget; I am talking about all things media-related. My family has not had cable in eight years. Yep, we have gone almost a decade without cable and we love it. However, whenever we are hanging out at our neighbor's house watching college football, I am reminded of how media can wreck a budget.

You are constantly being convinced by commercials to purchase things you can probably live without. Commercials are not the only thing at fault for convincing you to buy that super awesome mop; Facebook is to blame as well. All around us others are trying to convince us to spend money on items we "need."

Solution: Hold tight and keep accountable to your budget. If you think you are not being convinced by commercials or social media to wreck your budget, challenge yourself to a sixty-day fast. Have your cable suspended and cut yourself off from social media, and see if that has an impact on your spending.

3. Personality

If your budget does not match your personality, your budget will fail. My family can survive without going out to eat every week, but maybe that is something your family enjoys. Therefore, if you cut it out of your budget entirely, you may be setting yourself up for failure.

Solution: Instead of cutting dinning out completely, make room in your budget for a night out once or twice a month. That will allow your family to enjoy one of their favorite things while keeping your budget in check.

4. Denying that Bad Habit

If there is one thing that I hate to budget for, it is my hubs' cigarettes. I would much rather pretend that expense does not exist every week but it does. If I tried to deny how much we spent on cigarettes every month, my budget would not be accurate. Maybe you or your loved ones do not have a smoking addiction, but there might be something else that you would rather pretend did not exist - like a weekly Starbucks habit or bar tab.

Solution: We all have our vices, whatever they may be. If you aren't going to quit, you need to recognize it and put it in the budget.

5. Black Hole

Is there a major expense that is eating up too much of your budget? If so, you will find yourself coming up short every month and failing at saving enough money for your emergency fund. Examples of these major "black hole" expenses are housing payments, car payments, and excessively high expenses like a vacation home.

Solution: Look at your housing payment and figure out the math if your payment is higher than what it should be. If you always underspend on your housing, you will be able to afford a manageable life. Do not overspend on your home or car; they are not worth it.

Here is the formula for making sure your mortgage or rent payment does not exceed 30 percent of your income:

Take Home Pay x 0.3 = Max Monthly Mortgage/Rent Payment

6. Covering Shortfalls

If you are consistently covering your shortfalls every month by borrowing money, you are wrecking your budget. Borrowing money can mean you are using credit cards, asking others for money, taking an advance (from paycheck or credit cards), and even using your emergency fund to cover costs that are not emergency related (hint: a new washing machine is not an emergency; it is a luxury). Borrowing money is essentially robbing Peter to pay Paul; you are taking money out of one pot and putting it into another without first thinking of how you are going to replenish the first pot once it is empty.

Solution: Do yourself and your budget a favor by being consistent in your spending.

7. Lack of Discipline

If you want your budget to work, you have to work on your self-discipline and follow your budget. No one else but you can make your budget better; there is no secret sauce or cure-all miracle to budgeting. It takes a lot of discipline and trial and error to make it work. Make it work.

Solution: If you find yourself struggling with sticking to your budget each month, sit down and re-work it. Your budget may need to be adjusted here and there as you figure out what works best for your family and your lifestyle. However, if you are completely ignoring your budget in certain spending categories, you may need to consider a cash-envelope system or some other method of monetary control. Changing a life-time of bad spending habits can be difficult! But you can make it work! Remind yourself of why you wanted to follow a budget; post your goals and share them with friends. Ask others to help keep you accountable.

The seven budget breakers above are by no means the only ways you might be hurting your budget; but they are some of the more common issues. The easiest way to figure out how you may be wrecking your budget is to take an honest look at how your budget performs every month and to identify any potential budget wreckers.

Challenge 4: Identify Your Budget Wreckers

Sit down and take a hard look at how the flow of money works in your household. What is causing you to fail at sticking to your budget? Is it the same issue every month or is it something that creeps up on you? Write down these potential budget wreckers and remember to keep them in mind (and in the budget) when you create your budget every month or week.

For example, some people forget to include a budget for items like gifts. Every month you may find yourself having to spend an unexpected $20 here or there for a birthday or baby shower; then in the summer months you feel as though you are buying wedding presents almost every weekend! If you didn't budget for incidental expenses like this, your budget would take a beating. Be honest with yourself about how to handle situations such as these. You may feel completely comfortable cutting all gift-spending entirely; or you may decide that you'll have to cut your eating-out budget in half in order to accommodate giving. Either way, your budget has to be re-evaluated and adjusted.

DITCH THE SPENDING HABIT

"The speed of your success is limited only by your dedications and what you're willing to sacrifice."

Nathan W. Morris

I truly believe that temptation is the root of all evil, not money. Temptation can creep up on even the most financially perceptive people and wreak havoc on their money plans. Although there will always be some level of temptation around, there are a few ways that you can remove it from your life. The best way I have found to do this is to practice "stop, think, buy."

Before you head to a cash register, stop, think about the item and the amount you are about to spend, and then buy if you still feel you need it. These are a few ways to make removing the temptation to head straight to the register a little easier.

Just Say No

Say no to impulse buys! They are the main culprit when it comes to wrecking budgets. You might just pop-in to the gas station to use the restroom, but before you know it you've grabbed a few donuts and a cup of coffee. Make yourself aware of the temptation to impulse buy by asking yourself, "Do I need this? Does it help me accomplish my goals?" Chances are it does neither.

Dining Out

Going out to eat can be such a treat, but only when treated as such. Far too often, we go out to eat on a regular basis and then wonder why our budgets and waistlines are out of shape. Work on making dining out a special treat instead of a regular occurrence. Maybe go out only once a month versus every weekend. Instead of eating lunch at fast food restaurants, make copy-cat recipes of your favorite meals and bring them to work with you. Chances are you will enjoy your homemade version better.

Inbox Clutter

Clean out your email's inbox and hit the unsubscribe button. Getting rid of all of those tempting email subscriptions from retailers will eliminate a lot of temptation. It is far too easy to spend money that was not planned when you are constantly bombarded with advertisements.

Online Window Shopping

Instead of just aimlessly browsing the internet or playing on Facebook before bed, read a book or enjoy some snuggle time with your significant other. Online window shopping is more dangerous to your budget than the old school method of window shopping because the shop is available to you twenty-four seven through that computer screen. When you do shop online, make a list of what you need and avoid purchasing anything that is not on the list.

I fell victim to this a couple of weeks ago when I purchased a book from Amazon on impulse with the "1-click purchase" button. Make yourself aware of how tempting this is and do what I did the next day when I was having buyer's remorse – remove your payment information from the sites you frequent. Next time you are shopping on that website, you'll have to go grab your wallet and manually input your card information, which will allow you a little time to think about the purchase before making it.

Manage Your Time

Make it a point to limit the amount of time you spend on social media. Letting go of the Facebook trend of aimlessly scrolling through my newsfeed every five minutes was one of the best decision I ever made, not just for my time but also for my budget. Facebook and other social media outlets are littered with ads from retailers for the next best deal of the century. Limiting the amount of time you spend on those sites will help you avoid the temptation to impulse buy.

Recognize your spending triggers so you can take control and avoid temptation when it inevitably creeps up on you. Learning how to say "no" to yourself is something that all adults must learn to do; we are in control of how much we allow temptation to dictate our budgets. Remember to stop, think, and then buy before making any purchase and you will make sticking to your budget easier.

Challenge 5: Stop. Think. Buy

Put into practice the stop, think, and buy method. Before making any purchases, stop and think about if you really need to make the purchase and if it is in your budget. If the purchase is something truly needed and is budgeted for, go ahead and buy it! However, if it is not, put it back, and walk away.

THE SPENDER VS. THE SAVER

"Marriage is about love; divorce is about money.

Anonymous

Which one are you, are you the spender or the saver? In my marriage, I am the saver and my hubs is the spender. Throughout our five years of marriage, this has resulted in many disagreements and excessively blown-out-of-portion arguments.

Chances are you have a similar predicament in your relationship; after all, opposites attract. My husband has blown through over a $100 a week before just in eating out and over $1,000 on one of his many home projects. I could beat him over the head, scream, and yell until my heart's content, but what would that really solve?

Nothing.

Personal finance is *personal* and it can get hairy when you throw another person who has a different financial perspective than you do in the mix. Over the course of our marriage, my husband and I have had to work through some serious issues, and many of them have been money related.

In order to keep the peace and the happiness flowing in our marriage, I have had to come up with a few ways of dealing with my hubs' spending habits. But, before I share them, I want to caution you that if your marriage is already suffering, whether entirely money-related or not, you may need to seek professional help from a marriage counselor to work through your relationship issues.

Strengths

What are your spouse's strengths when it comes to money? Does he spend hours searching for the best possible deal? Is she a master at clipping coupons? Consider the positive attributes of your spouse's spending habits so when you bring up the issues, you are not attacking them. Starting the conversation off on a positive note helps to keep the conversation productive and less argumentative; this allows you to reach a better resolution. (If you cannot find anything positive about their money habits, find something positive about another area of your lives. Are they great at getting the kids to eat their dinner or helping you around the house?)

Communicate

This is the key to a successful marriage in my book. I am not a pro at this thing called love but as a child of a divorced family, I can attest that communication is the key to a successful relationship. In order to have financial peace in your home, you have to communicate your concerns and issues with each other.

A couple of years ago, I made a huge budgeting mistake. A really bad one. It almost completely wiped out our savings. I was so upset with myself and I did not know how I was going to tell my husband, who I was constantly yelling at all the time for making us go over budget, that I was the one to blame this time. It was difficult to muster up the courage to tell him what I had done, but it brought us closer together because we had to find a solution, together. He was not happy about the mistake but he forgave me, which reminded me of how often I was failing to forgive him for his money mistakes.

Forgiveness

As I just mentioned above, you have to and need to forgive your spouse when they overspend. If you are communicating effectively with one another, you have to make sure you continually make it comfortable for your spouse to come to you when they have made a mistake. By offering your forgiveness when they do, you have a better chance of making your money work for you.

If there is true dishonesty happening when it comes to disclosing how money is being spent, it may be time to turn to outside help. Counseling can be a huge benefit to your marriage and your finances, even if your counselor is just a trusted friend. Make it a point to seek help together and remember to avoid the blame game. Admitting your marriage needs help is not easy and throwing blame into the mix only sours the deal even more.

Make a Plan

Making a plan may seem like the first step in dealing with a spender of a spouse but in reality, it comes after the hard stuff. Before you can make a plan, and expect it to work, you have to figure each other's strengths out, communicate openly and honestly, and most importantly, be willing to offer forgiveness when needed. Once those have all been addressed, then you can sit down and make out your plan.

Create your budget together, or if your spender is like mine, you create the budget and allow them to view the budget and have veto power over it. Give them a copy of the budget so they will know what and where they are allowed to spend money.

One of the most effective ways I am able to combat my husband's spending problem is by reminding him of our savings plan. Create a savings plan together and remind each other of it often, especially when tempted to spend money that is not part of your plan. It is never easy to hear someone point out where you have failed but remember that you two are in this thing together.

Challenge 6: Communicate Openly, Offer Forgiveness, and Create a Plan

In order to succeed with money, you must play on the same team as your spouse. Make it a point to communicate often and openly about your finances, your own spending habits, and most importantly about your spouse's strengths. Offer your forgiveness when your spouse spends money outside the budget or makes a financial error, no matter how large the mistake is.

Your challenge is to make speaking with love, kindness, and forgiveness part of your financial vocabulary. Set an appointment with your spouse to create your budget together and to get on the same page as each other so you can work towards the same financial goals.

It takes a while to figure out the best way to make your budget meetings work, but keep trying. My husband works crazy hours, which makes setting an appointment with him for a budget meeting difficult. Therefore, when his hours are crazy and a budget meeting is nearly impossible, I set up the budget, email it to him, and he responds with his changes. Figure out a way to make budget meetings work with you and your spouse. You are a team and you need to be playing on the same field.

STOP LIVING PAYCHECK TO PAYCHECK

"I don't live paycheck to paycheck. I live paycheck to four days before paycheck."

Anonymous

Half payments work incredibly well to help you find financial peace. In fact, half payments are the only reason why my family was able to stop living paycheck to paycheck. The half payment method is where you take a regularly occurring payment, such as a $300 car payment, and divide it in half. You then set aside that money (half of the total bill) at the beginning of the month, and take the rest out when you send out the payment. This will ensure that you have the full payment ready-to-go come payment due date. To clarify, I am suggesting taking the half payment and setting it aside, not sending it in to your creditor. However, if your creditor accepts half payments made before the due date and paying the money immediately would benefit you, do it.

If that seems confusing, here is a little break down of how it works if you receive a bi-monthly paycheck. (I am still using the $300 car payment example from above):

>Paycheck #1: $600

>Half payment for car payment: $150

>Total left from paycheck #1: $450

>Paycheck #2: $600

>Half payment for car payment: $150

>Total left from paycheck #2: $450

What is the purpose behind using this system? What if instead of using half payments, we look at this example of how it usually plays out for most:

>Paycheck #1: $600

>No half payment

>Total left from paycheck #1: $600

Paycheck #2: $600

No half payment

Full car payment: $300

Total left from paycheck #2: $300

Some may think that option #2 seems fine, and essentially, there is nothing wrong with it. The issue with the second option is that you now have lost an additional $150 from paycheck #2. Of course, the argument is that you gain $300 to paycheck #1, but do you really gain that money? What usually happens when there is money just left on the table? It typically becomes absorbed somewhere else in your spending because, subconsciously, the money is still available.

If, instead, you used half payments, you would manage to have your full car payment every month without having to scrape by at the end of the month. You would end up with more money in your pocket over time and your finances would become easier to manage, lessening your financial stress.

This system will work no matter how often you are paid. If you are paid once a month, consider starting the half payment method by only making quarter payments or small payments every week. Once again, I suggest starting with the smallest fixed bill every month as this is usually an easier place to start and will prevent you from feeling overwhelmed.

The half payment method is exactly how I managed to stop living paycheck to paycheck and how I was able to pull myself out of financial trouble all those years ago. It definitely works, though it can be challenging at first. It will bless you in the end by making managing your money easier.

Challenge 7: Make Half Payments

Start using the half payment method for all your regularly occurring payments. Start with your lowest regular payment and divide it in half. Use the half payment method with that payment until you develop the habit. Then start the half payment method with your next lowest regular payment and continue the trend with all your regular payments.

BUILD AN EMERGENCY FUND

"Saving money isn't about being able to buy bigger and better things. It's about being prepared to take care of your family."

Dave Ramsey

After you have created your budget and identified habits that may derail you, it is time to start working on building an emergency fund. Dave Ramsey teaches that you should start with a $1,000 emergency fund before paying off debt. My husband did not agree with Dave's $1,000 figure. He believed the amount should be higher, but he did not have a specific number in mind. Therefore, we had to compromise at $1,500 as our starting point. You can pick the amount you want to build up to. Just remember to keep this amount realistic. There is no point in attempting to build an emergency fund if it will take you ten years to build it. Likewise, you should have enough money in your fund to cover true emergencies. Remember, emergencies can happen at any time and any place.

The easy way to start building your emergency fund is to make it as out-of-sight, out-of-mind as possible. When my husband and I started building ours, I calculated five percent of my husband's paychecks and set up an automatic withdraw every week to go towards our emergency fund. This kept me from inevitably forgetting to put the money away and spending it elsewhere.

Our emergency fund is not with our regular bank. Keeping with the out-of-sight, out-of-mind mentality, we opened a savings account with Capital One 360 to house our emergency fund. Not being able to see this money whenever we log into our regular bank account to view our statements keeps us from being tempted to dip into the account whenever we hit a little bump in the road.

The key to winning with your emergency fund is to keep it for emergencies only. Your dishwasher breaking is not an emergency. Your spouse losing his or her job is an emergency. The idea behind the emergency fund is to have at least six months' worth of income for your household put aside. This way, if you or your spouse becomes unemployed, your family can stay afloat while seeking new employment.

An emergency fund will provide you with a peace of mind unlike any other. Knowing that you have a cushion to fall back on will make it easier if you hit a huge bump in the road.

Challenge 8: Build an Emergency Fund

Right now, before you can think too much about it, figure out what five percent of yours or your spouse's paycheck is. Open an account with a bank separate from your regular bank and set up an automatic withdraw from every paycheck for that amount to be applied to your emergency fund. Some employers do offer the option of automatically withdrawing a designated percentage from your paycheck to a separate account. My only word of caution with this is to make sure that the account the funds are being allocated to is the best one for your money and is earning you the best possible interest rate.

Now, forget that account exists! Your emergency fund is not money that you can play with or buy Christmas presents with. That money is specifically for emergencies only; do whatever is in your power to keep yourself from touching that money unless it is a true emergency. It is important to note that an emergency fund is imperative to your overall financial well-being and should be established before attempting to pay off debt, go on vacation, or make any large purchases. The purpose of the emergency fund is to protect you against Murphy's Law.

When you reach your set amount in your emergency fund, the next step is to decide if you will stop or lower your contribution amount. The reason behind doing this is so you can allocate the funds towards something else like paying off debt, saving for your children's education, or saving for a large purchase.

DUMP THE DEBT

"People who understand interest earn it. People that don't, pay it."

                Anonymous

I know this is a tough one for many. Debt is comfortable; it is familiar, and heck, most people we know carry some type of debt. But what if you no longer had debt? Imagine if the only money you had to pay every month was for utilities, insurance, groceries, savings, and whatever fun money you wanted to pay for.

Sounds amazing, doesn't it? It is possible to slay the debt monster and to start living an amazing life free of the stranglehold of debt. I am not 100 percent debt-free yet, but I will be. In my very short time on this earth, I have paid off over $40,000 of debt and currently am on track to pay off just over $20,000 of debt this year.

It is possible to pay off debt, save money, live life on a budget, and actually *live* life. It isn't easy, but nothing worthwhile ever is. So how do you do it? How do you pay off debt when you are still living off debt? You hustle.

Make a Plan

Your specific debt payoff plan will probably look different from your neighbors' – you are different people using debt differently. Avoid comparing your success or failures to others; they are using a different road map than you.

To develop your debt payoff plan you will need to first determine how much debt you actually have. Make a list of all the debts you have: their balances, interest rates, minimum payment amounts, and due dates. Debts you should record on this list include credit cards, student loans, car loans, any other type of personal loans you may have, and your mortgage. Your mortgage should always be last on the list as it should be the highest debt balance and your best asset.

Choose a Method

Once you know how much you owe, decide how you are going to tackle your debt. There are two general methods you can choose from: the snowball method and the debt consolidation method.

The debt snowball method is where you take the lowest debt and work to pay it off first. Once that debt is paid off, you apply the amount you were paying to that debt towards the debt with the next lowest balance. You keep repeating this until all the debts are paid.

In order to keep yourself motivated to pay off your debt, keep your list of debts somewhere that you and your family can view it often. Every time you pay off a debt, cross it off your list and enjoy the sense of accomplish you'll get from your hard work.

If there is a debt that you can get rid of quickly, regardless of the amount of the debt, do it. For example, if you have a car loan that you will not be able to pay off in two years, consider selling the car and paying cash for an older used car. I know firsthand how difficult a decision this can be. I had to give up my full-loaded Tahoe with all the bells and whistles for a well-loved older car with busted speakers. It was a difficult choice but we managed to dump $18,000 of debt in one day because I came to terms with the fact that the Tahoe was simply a mode of transportation and did not define me as a person.

The debt consolidation method is a little more risky. If you are so deep in the red that you are near bankruptcy, debt consolidation can be a great way to help you get out of debt without filing for bankruptcy. However, using a debt consolidation service can look just as bad on your credit report as a bankruptcy so tread with caution. If you are considering using a debt consolidation service or debt consolidation loan, make sure you fully understand the terms and conditions of the agreement before you sign

Personally, I have had success using a debt consolidation loan to help pay off a portion of my debt. I had three credit cards with high balances and high interest rates. My annual income was $18,500 and there was no way I was going to make a dent in those debts without the interest killing me. Again, I caution you to only do this if you are in dire need of a way to get out of debt and to read the terms of the agreement carefully. Make sure the interest rate of the loan is lower than the interest rates of the debts you are trying to consolidate and make sure the payment is something you can easily afford. The goal is to pay off your debt, so you want to be able to pay more than the minimum payment every month in order to dig yourself out of debt.

Challenge 9: Determine Your Debt Payoff Plan

Make a list of all the debts you have, in order from the lowest balance to the highest. Take note of the interest rates, due dates, and the minimum payments due every month. Determine what debts you can get rid of quickly (think car and jewelry loans) and determine if you are going to use the debt snowball method or if you need to use the debt consolidation method. Remember if you are married, you must do this together with your spouse. Getting them on board may be tough, but chances are once you have a list of your debts and a timetable to pay them off they will jump on board.

Determine how much extra you can afford to pay every month towards your lowest balance debt. Post your list where you can see it every day and include the extra payment amount(s) in your budget. The next chapter covers ways to make more money in order to jump-start your debt payoff plan and emergency fund.

DEVELOP A POSITIVE CASH FLOW

"Unless you control your money, making more money won't help. You'll only have bigger payments."

Dave Ramsey

Before you can get out of debt or build an emergency fund, you need a positive cash flow. You will not succeed in paying off your debt if you do not first have a positive flow of money every month.

Back when I was struggling with my debt, I had zero positive cash flow for the month because my bills and minimum payments were taking all of my cash. I had to put groceries and fuel for my car on credit because I had absolutely no cash to purchase them with.

It is crucial that you wait to start attacking the debt monster until after you have started your emergency fund. Developing a positive cash flow is not only beneficial in paying off your debt but will also help you build up your emergency fund faster.

This is where the concept of paying yourself first comes in. You pay yourself first by putting money away in your emergency fund, retirement, investment accounts, or other savings before applying money elsewhere.

If you are struggling as I was with zero cash flow, you will have to work hard, and by hard, I mean you will have to work your tail off. You need to find ways to generate enough cash to throw into your emergency savings or debt payoff plan by:

- Selling items that you no longer use.

- Picking up extra hours at work.

- Getting a second job.

- Letting go of items that are costing you too much.

- Using tax refunds or other "free" money.

- Finding ways to save money on everyday expenses.

I started with selling off items I no longer needed and no longer used to jump-start my savings goal. I tore through my apartment finding all sorts of goodies that I could sell off. I did not make a large profit but it started the process.

I picked up extra hours at work when my office was remodeling and needed extra hands with painting and moving furniture. It was anything but fun but it helped me get a little bit closer to being able to breathe without feeling the weight of my financial burden.

I even got a second job for a short while. You do not need to work at a second job forever. Go into the job knowing that it is only temporary. Set a goal for yourself--once you reach it you can quit the second job. I only needed to work at the second job for a month before I was able to reach my goal and quit. Make sure you are kind enough to the employer to let them know that this is a temporary job for you.

There really is no such thing as "free" money but there is sometimes money that appears to be free. (Think bonus money from work, cash back earned from Ebates, Swagbucks, tax refund, etc.) It can be a great help towards reaching your savings and debt free goals. Start applying any and all extra money towards your goals as soon as you receive it.

Lastly, you can start trying to save money on your everyday expenses by calling your utility providers, cutting coupons, meal planning, or hand-making some commonly used items. Saving money can sometimes be no fun but it is a means to an end, not the end itself when trying to build your savings and slaying the debt monster.

Take control of your money and start bringing your money out of the red by having a positive cash flow. This is where the debt-free journey starts. Without a positive flow of money, your debt-free journey will fail before you even leave the starting line.

Challenge 10: Take baby steps towards building a positive cash flow

Gather up any items you have that are no longer being used and are still in great condition. Start selling these items on sites like Craigslist, eBay, and Facebook yard sale sites. If you find selling items online difficult, host a yard sale with a friend or neighbor in order to earn cash for your stuff. Another great option is to use consignment sales and online consignment shops like thredUP. However, most consignment sales and shops only accept name brand items so if the majority of your clothing is not name brand, it may be best to stick with a yard sale or sell your stuff online yourself.

Once you have received payment for your items, immediately apply that money towards either your emergency fund or your debt in order to get your savings and snowball payments rolling. If you wait too long to apply it, you will more than likely end up spending the money on something else.

Start earning "free" money on sites like Swagbucks.com and InboxDollars.com in order to apply the cash towards your debt or emergency savings fund. I have personally used both sites to fund our debt-free Christmases for the last three years and used my Swagbucks earnings to pay off a creditor. You will also want to start applying any money you receive in the form of a work bonus or tax refund towards your debt and emergency fund.

Once you start applying these different methods, you will start generating a positive cash flow each month. This will help to stabilize your budget and allow you to have more room to breathe each month.

BREAKING BAD MONEY HABITS

"Change is painful. Few people have the courage to seek out change. Most people won't change until the pain of where they are exceeds the pain of change."

Dave Ramsey, *The Total Money Makeover*

We all have bad habits, especially when it comes to money. We have spending triggers that cause us to spend money unnecessarily and we have wants. Breaking bad money habits is essential to sticking to and managing a household budget.

> Do you keep a budget in your head instead of writing it down?
>
> Do you have a vice that is draining your budget (smoking, drinking, gambling, retail therapy shopping, etc)?
>
> Do you only pay the minimum payment on your credit cards?
>
> Do you keep putting off calling your utility providers to reduce your monthly expenses?
>
> Do you keep premium channels but only watch seven channels?
>
> Do you tend to shop out of boredom or as "retail therapy?"
>
> Are you underinsured?

These are only a few of the possible bad money habits we can develop over time. Determine what your bad money habit is and work towards breaking it.

You can determine your bad money habits by looking over your budget and figuring out where you keep spending your money, or you can ask someone close to you what your bad money habits are. Once you have determined your habits, take ownership of them! Then, figure out how you can avoid these habits, and set a reminder to work diligently to stop this habit.

If your bad money habit is a vice, seek help stopping this bad habit. My husband is a smoker and I understand how difficult it is to quit a vice; if the vice is something that you truly want to stop, seek help. If the vice is something that you are not ready to let go of yet, pick another bad habit to break first.

Baby steps. Remember that it takes baby steps to reach any goal - including breaking bad habits and developing new, better ones.

If you are really struggling with breaking a bad money habit, replace it with a good money habit. For example, if you consistently blow your budget purchasing lattes from Starbucks, start purchasing gourmet coffee at the grocery store and brewing your own at home. Or add salt to cheaper coffee to make it taste better (it really does work!).

Whatever your bad habits are, take ownership of them and start working towards letting them go today. Your budget will thank you.

Challenge 11: Breaking Bad

There is a theory that it takes twenty-one days to either break a habit or form a new one. Take the next twenty-one days to break one bad money habit and replace it with a good money habit. Use a spreadsheet to track your progress breaking this bad money habit.

Once the twenty-one days are over and you have successfully broken yourself of this bad money habit, pick another bad money habit to work on for the next twenty-one days. Keep repeating this process until you are comfortable that you have successfully eliminated all your bad money habits.

Make sure to check in on your money habits periodically to ensure that no new bad money habits have developed. If they have, start the twenty-one day process over again until you no longer have those bad money habits.

DON'T BE CHEAP

"A bargain ain't a bargain if it is not something that you need."

      Sidney Carroll

This is going to muddy the water for some. It is okay to be cheap sometimes but really, you should strive to be frugal, not cheap.

With the Great Recession came a need for many families to change their mindsets from "buy, buy, buy" to "save, save, save" in order to keep a roof over their heads. Maybe you became a *frugalista* because you or your husband lost your jobs.

But, is living a frugal lifestyle really that easy? Are all of those people claiming to be "frugal" really just being cheap? Do frugal and cheap go hand in hand? Sometimes, yes because shopping for deals and using coupons are simply *a part* of frugal living but they are not the means of living frugally. That is the difference between being a cheapskate and being a frugalista. There is a big difference between purchasing items you do not need simply because they are on sale and forgoing the purchase because it does not add value to your life.

According to Mr. Webster, these are the definitions of frugal and cheap:

> Frugal: characterized by or reflecting economy in the use of resources
>
> Cheap: not costing a lot of money: of low quality: not worth a lot of money

Hmmmm…so there is a difference!

Being frugal does not mean that you are simply couponing, looking for the latest and greatest sale, or scoring something for free; it is a lifestyle characterized by making the most out of your current resources.

Truthfully, when I was spending credit as if it were going out of style, I was actually just being cheap. I only purchased items on sale or with a coupon, but I was buying things that were not going to last just because they were a good price! Overall, I was just accumulating more junk with little value.

I grew up in a frugal home; my mom is a daughter of parents who grew up during the Great Depression and passed down their frugal ways to their five children. I remember thinking that my mom was cheap because we could not purchase something if it was not either on sale, with a coupon, or at the very least in the budget. Instead of purchasing Halloween costumes, we made them. I remember turning a concert dress (I played the flute) into a witch's dress by cutting it up to make it look ragged and sewing ribbons and chiffon in random places. It drove me crazy as a kid, but now I get it.

My mom was a lunch lady raising two children on a very small salary. Being frugal was her only option. My mom is still the most frugal woman on the planet even with an empty nest, but I know that she will retire well and that her children will not have to bear the financial burden of caring for her.

Frugal living is a mindset and it is not for everyone. Frugal living means that you look at what you have and make the most of it. Before making a purchase, I always ask myself if I have anything at home that I could use instead of buying this new item. Usually, the answer is yes. For example, I really wanted to add something to our mantel because it was looking a little bare. In Target one day, I saw some gorgeous bottles on sale that I thought would look perfect on our mantel. I had a Cartwheel coupon and immediately I put those bottles in the cart. As I walked around to grab the items that were actually on my list, I thought about those bottles. Even with my coupon and the sale, I was going to be paying almost $40 for them!

I just could not do it. Instead, I decided to put the bottles back and see what I had at home. I raided our liquor cabinet and found three bottles that worked just as well. I ended up not spending any money at all by decorating with items I already had in the house.

That is the frugal mindset. Instead of purchasing something on sale, or even at the thrift store, you first look to what you already have and make use of it first.

Challenge 12: Cheap or Frugal?

If you find yourself purchasing things simply because they are on sale or you have a coupon, I challenge you to stop. Instead, try to only shop sales and with coupons for items you actually need and use. I challenge you to first look through your entire home for items that could be used in place of the things that you are planning on purchasing.

You may be surprised during this challenge how much money you will save just by not shopping. Start changing your mindset from cheap to frugal.

MONEY MINUTE

"The person who doesn't know where his next dollar is coming from usually doesn't know where his last dollar went."

Anonymous

How many times do you review your finances? Do you review them daily, weekly, monthly, or yearly? Maybe you review them a couple of different times throughout the week or many even a few times a day.

One of the quickest ways to get a handle on your finances is to have a "money minute" every day. This sixty-second window can be in the morning or at night – whenever you feel you will have the time to carve out one whole minute. For me personally, this minute is during my boys' naptime when I can actually hear myself think.

What exactly is a money minute?

Take a "money minute" to log in to your bank(s) or whatever budgeting software program you use and review your transactions from either the previous day or that day (the time of day you have your money minute will determine what transactions you are reviewing).

Why is a money minute important?

A money minute is important because it allows you to see where your money is actually going. Keeping track of your expenses is great as long as you do it consistently or else you will lose track. During your money minute every day, you can use this time to track only one-day's transactions making it easier to account for your expenses.

This is also a great time to catch any errors made by your bank (fees, incorrect withdrawals, missing deposits, etc.) and an even better time to catch fraud or identity theft.

Will a money minute help with budgeting?

Yes! Absolutely this will help with your budgeting process. It is one of the many elements of building a budget that works.

Carving out time for a money minute every day makes sticking to your budget so much easier because you are not waiting until the end of the week (or month) to check in on your budget. You are taking care of things when they occur instead of scrambling after the fact to figure out where your money went and why your budget did not work.

What do I do exactly during my money minute?

During my money minute, I write down in my expense tracker all of the day's expenses rounded up to the nearest dollar. I look over my expenses to determine what budget categories they fall into and take note of their totals. I then review where I am currently in those categories of my budget – have I gone over, am I close to going over? If I have gone over, I can then easily review the transactions to determine where/why I went over and adjust my budget as necessary.

Your process may look different depending on how you budget, but the money minute should be used to track your expenses, determine any errors/discrepancies, and readjust your budget as needed. This is a great way to help stop spending money when you realize that you have already reached or exceeded the amount for a certain budget category – no more waiting until the end of the month to figure it all out!

A money minute is an essential tool for making your budget work and for getting a handle on your spending. Use this tool to make your budgeting process easier and more efficient.

Challenge 13: Make Time for a Money Minute

Start today with your sixty-second window of financial opportunity. Carve out a regular time each day to review your day's transactions to ensure that everything is in tip-top-shape. Remember from our breaking habits chapter that it typically takes twenty-one days to develop a new habit. Therefore, make sure you stick to making your money minute a part of your daily activities.

GET A HANDLE ON UNEXPECTED EXPENSES

"Beware of the little expenses; a small leak will sink a great ship."

      Benjamin Franklin

Unexpected expenses can be the ultimate downfall to a family's finances. They go hand-in-hand with Murphy's Law and they are the biggest complaint when it comes to budgeting. Many people give up trying to budget all together when faced with unexpected expenses repeatedly. Giving up will not solve anything; keep budgeting and put these tips into practice to help make unexpected expenses more manageable.

Plan

Yes, there are some expenses that are flat-out unexpected. However, most "unexpected" expenses can and should be expected. One example is medical expenses. Most medical-related expenses should be planned for. If you go into the emergency room, for whatever reason, you should know what percentage of the final bill you will be responsible for paying. Even if you do not know the exact total of the emergency room visit, you should be prepared and you should know ahead of time what your insurance policy covers and does not cover.

Another example is car repairs. Many people act like all car repairs are unexpected but truthfully, if you drive a car regularly, it will need repairs at some point. It will need regular oil changes and maintenance. It will need new tires. It will wear out and need replacement parts. These should be expected and planned for. You should also always have your auto insurance deductible saved and ready-to-go should you become involved in an accident.

Cushion

Ensure you are ready to take on unexpected expenses by allowing extra cushion in your budget categories. You know that the car will need repairs from time-to-time but how often? My husband is a road warrior; he drives his own truck for work, and puts many miles on his truck every year. We know to expect, every year, that we will have to put new tires on his truck. And because he *does* travel so much, we purchase high-quality tires to ensure that we are getting the most out of our money. Knowing and being prepared every year for this expense keeps us from having to reach for a credit card to make this hefty purchase every few months.

Put as much extra money as you can into your budget categories to ensure that the money will be there when you inevitably need it. If you are struggling to find wiggle room in your budget, you may need to find ways to increase your income (selling off used items, taking on a side job, etc).

Emergency Fund

An emergency fund is not a fund to purchase a new washer and dryer with; it is a fund designed to keep you afloat when a true emergency strikes, such as your home's breadwinner losing his or her job. Plan for the unexpected by keeping a well-funded emergency fund at all times, period.

An emergency fund is a must have to combat unexpected expenses. It will provide you the cushion you need to be prepared for life's bumps in the road.

Remember to plan, prepare, and then execute when the inevitable "unexpected" expense arises and you will be able to avoid going into debt to pay for the expense.

Challenge 14: Prepare for Unexpected Expenses

Make a list of all of the foreseeable expenses your family may incur. If you drive a vehicle regularly, write down routine maintenance items like oil changes, brake pad replacements, new tires, and your auto insurance deductible. If you own your own home, write down home maintenance items such as roof repairs,

HVAC system repairs, and your home insurance deductible. Write down any possible medical bills that you may incur. If you suffer from a chronic illness that may result in an unexpected stay in the hospital, make sure you write that down, too. Write down your health insurance deductible and how much your health insurance company will cover of your medical bills.

It is imperative that you have your deductibles (auto, home, and medical) saved and ready to go should disaster strike. Make it part of your financial goals to have savings accounts designated for these deductibles and only touch that money when you need to pay your deductible.

DON'T BURDEN YOUR LOVED ONES

"To enjoy a long, comfortable retirement, save more today."

Suze Orman

As a parent, I know how tempting it is to spoil your children. You want to give them everything, to give them the amazing life that you didn't have. You work hard for your money and in return, you lavish fun things, fun toys, new clothes, or new experiences on your children (or maybe even your grandchildren).

However, you could be overlooking one very big burden you may be placing on your children – you. You can easily become a burden on your children later in life if you are not prepared. Do you have a retirement account? Do you have a savings account? What exactly is your savings plan and what are your financial goals? These are important questions to ask *now*, even if you just found out that you are pregnant with your first child.

I know that as a mom the last thing that I ever want to be is a burden on my children or grandchildren. Yes, there may come a time when I cannot physically take care of myself anymore and I may need my children to help with basic needs. However, I do not want my children to have to struggle to pay for my care. I want to know that they will not have to bear the financial burden of taking care of an aging parent who carelessly blew money away for years without saving.

It is okay for your children to go without the latest and greatest new gadget, toy, or trendy outfit. They may not be happy about it but they are certainly not underprivileged. If you are spending more money than you are saving for retirement, you are putting your children at risk now for having to take care of you later.

I know some believe that they will never live to see retirement. That may very well be true, however, what if something happened to you right now? What if you died right now, do you have life insurance; do you have money in savings and retirement that could possibly go to your children at a designated time in their lives? These are important questions to ask yourself and to discuss with your spouse.

If you are worried about providing your children with the life you never had growing up, make sure you are not setting them up for financial hardships later in life. The financial habits you teach your children today will affect their futures. For example, both my brother and I have owned more cars in our short existence on this earth than our almost 65-year-old mother. Our daddy unfortunately taught us that what made you successful was the ability to have a new car every year. Do not get me wrong--my daddy did not intend to teach us that lesson, but every year we watched him get a new car and heard him say how great it felt to do so. When we got older, we followed his example. This ended up creating an endless cycle of debt for both my brother and I.

Save for retirement now; do not wait for tomorrow because it may already be gone. Saving now ensures that not only you are covered when you reach retirement, but also that your children and grandchildren may inherent money from you, which is a true financial blessing to those that are raised in a financially savvy household.

If you are one of the many Americans facing retirement without any money saved, you need to put into action an aggressive retirement savings strategy immediately. If you are employed at a company where a 401(k) is offered, take advantage of any employer matching and contribute the maximum percentage allowed. If you are self-employed, open a Roth IRA and start contributing at least six percent of your income each pay period towards your Roth IRA account.

How close you are to retiring will determine how much money you need to save in order to ensure that you have enough saved to avoid burdening your family later down the road. Do not simply think of your retirement account as money for your future self to live off of; think of it as money to pay for your needs should you need hospice care or need to stay in a nursing home facility.

As important as retirement savings are, you may not be able to start building your retirement fund right away. Once you have built up your emergency fund and started your debt snowball, then it's time to start thinking of the future you and the future of your family.

Challenge 15: Save for Retirement

If you currently have a retirement account, seek a financial professional that can help you determine how much money you will have when you retire based on your age and current contribution to your account. A million dollars may seem like a lot of money now, but think about it this way: if you currently make $50,000 a year, retire with only a million dollars at the age of 65, and continue living the lifestyle you are used to, you will only have enough yearly salary for twenty years. You will be 85 years old when the money runs out.

If you do not currently have a retirement fund, start one. If you are employed ask your Human Resources department if your company offers a 401(k) plan and if they offer employer matching. If yes, take advantage of this free money and contribute the maximum percentage allowed. If you are self-employed or your employer does not offer a 401(k) package, open a Roth IRA and start contributing. Seek out a financial professional to review your contributions to tell you how much you should contribute in order to reach your financial goals.

Make sure you are financially prepared for retirement and schedule an appointment with a banker or financial professional that can help you decide on the best retirement options for *you*.

APPLY THE 50/20/30 FRAMEWORK

"Don't tell me what you value, show me your budget, and I'll tell you what you value."

Joe Biden

Now that you have grown accustom to using the basic budget that you set up in Chapter Three, it is time to revamp that budget to maximize your money. Budget categories usually cause headaches and can be very confusing, but this simple approach to budget categories will help you figure out if you are spending too much in one area and not enough in another. It is all about finding balance.

One of the simplest ways to set up your budget is to follow the principle of 50/20/30. It is not at all as complicated as it sounds; in fact, I believe it makes budgeting a whole lot easier.

>50 percent is for your essentials

>20 percent is for your future

>30 percent is for your lifestyle

>Let us break this down a little further.

50

Your essentials are what you need to survive. Essentials are your food, shelter, and transportation to work (in order to earn money to provide for the essentials). Fifty percent of your total monthly income should go towards these basic survival needs. This is why it is imperative that you avoid overpaying on your home, utilities, and transportation. Spending too much on those items will not leave you much money for groceries and other household essentials. Make sure when you budget this category that you are not overpaying on your utilities every month.

Avoid spending too much on your essentials. Living in a home you cannot afford or one that eats up too much of your money every month will make it difficult to enjoy the fruits of your labor. Keep this budget category in check so you can actually have fun with your money.

20

Your future is your debt repayment, emergency fund, investments, and retirement savings. How you decide to allocate twenty percent of your total monthly income to these categories is dependent upon where you are in life and what your financial goals are. For example, if you are attempting to pull yourself out of debt, a huge portion of your twenty percent is going to go towards your debt repayment plan. If your retirement account needs a little love, a large portion of your twenty percent will go towards your 401(k) or IRA accounts. If you have no savings, then the majority, if not all of your twenty percent will go towards building your emergency fund.

30

Your lifestyle consists of the things that you enjoy spending money on like travel, eating out, gifts, and shopping. This category is the first to go when you are in financial trouble; do not get caught up in the thirty percent outweighing your future. This account is intended to make living life fun but life will not be enjoyable if you are struggling to pay your monthly bills. Before planning this category of your budget, make sure your essentials and future are balanced before you play.

Remember that you must first apply the fifty percent, then twenty percent, and then the thirty percent. It is tempting to want to apply this category first; try to avoid that temptation as the more balanced your first two categories are, the easier and more stress-free it is to live your lifestyle of choice.

How you decide to divide the individual categories is up to you. These individual percentages will look different for everyone. Personal finance is personal and although money connects us, it works differently for each of us.

Challenge 16: Apply the 50/20/30 framework to your basic budget

Review the basic budget you made earlier in this book and apply the 50/20/30 framework. Remember to start with fifty, then move on to twenty, and then apply the thirty. It is okay if your framework is a little unbalanced; the ultimate goal is to balance your budget to be as close to the 50/20/30 framework as possible.

STICK TO IT

"Our greatest weakness lies in giving up. The most certain way to succeed is always to try just one more time."

        Thomas A. Edison

This is the most difficult step in living a real life on a budget – sticking to it. If you have made it this far in the book, you are one step closer to sticking to your budget because you have decided to take ownership of your money. The basic budget in challenge three is the one that I credit as saving my life. When I was deep in financial despair and felt no hope and I just wanted to give up, I sat down and wrote out a basic budget. When I did, I saw just how in the red I was. It is a scary thing the moment that we realize we are to blame for our mistakes and we are the only ones that can change things. We spend countless hours and precious moments of our lives blaming others and wishing for saving grace all without accepting responsibility for our own actions.

It is not easy sticking to a budget and there may be times where you fail. When you do, give yourself grace; figure out where you went wrong, and try again. This is real life and it will not always go according to our perfectly laid plans.

Make a point to set up weekly and monthly budget meetings with your spouse in order to ensure that you are both on the same page. It is impossible to succeed with your new budget if you and your spouse are on different playing fields. Get on the same team, make a budget together, and stick to it together.

Strive to live a joyful *real life on a budget* and thrive by making your money work for you. You work hard to earn it, now make it work for you.

Challenge 17: Stick to Your Budget

No amount of information in the world will do you any good if you do not apply it. Go out and make sticking to your budget and managing your money a priority. Post your goals, budget, debt payoff plan, and savings plan somewhere that you and your family can see it every day to remind yourselves of what you are working towards. If you discover that something is not working, make the necessary adjustments so you can stick to your budget.

ABOUT THE AUTHOR

Jessi is the writer behind *The Budget Mama*, a personal finance website where she shares her family's real life on budget in all its gory details. Jessi is committed to helping her readers live and thrive on a budget. Her goal is to encourage others to become better money managers by sharing her real-world money advice and personal budget successes and failures.

Jessi is married to the handiest man around and is also the sleep-deprived mom of two wild little boys. She is the big sister of a U.S. Marine, and the daughter of a blue-collar man and the most frugal woman on the planet.

After failing with money in her early adult life, Jessi was determined to accept the challenge that God had given her and turn her life around. She and her husband paid off over $40,000 in debt before their thirtieth birthdays. They are still on their journey to debt freedom, but by accepting the challenges and lessons that God put in front of them, they have been able to overcome their obstacles.

Her vision is to inspire and encourage others on the road to financial freedom.

If you would like to connect with Jessi, you can find her here:

The Blog: www.thebudgetmama.com

Facebook: http://facebook.com/thebudgetmama

Twitter: @thebudgetmama

Instagram: @thebudgetmama

Pinterest: http://pinterest.com/thebudgetmama

Google +: https://plus.google.com/u/0/+JessiFearon

LinkedIn: https://www.linkedin.com/in/jessicafearon

Join her community here by signing up to receive her weekly email updates!

http://eepurl.com/bop6ir   or

Are you ready to build a budget that works and start making your money work for you?

Jessi's book, *Build a Budget that Works* is an easy-to-follow workbook designed to help you build a budget that works for your life. Complete with beautiful printable budget worksheets, *Build a Budget that Works* will guide you through the budgeting process and help you get started on your journey to financial success.

You can find *Build a Budget that Works* on Amazon here: http://amzn.to/1 5xUZ8M

ACKNOWLEDGEMENTS

This book project has had so many hands lift it up that there is no possible way to create a proper list for a proper thank-you. But thank you to all who have pushed and lifted this project from the first day.

Patrick Fearon, my first and only partner, advisor, best friend, and husband. Thank you for living this real life on a budget with me. You rock, hot stuff.

> **My Mastermind Team:**
> Toni of DebtFreeDivas.org
> Kim of ThriftyLittleMom.com
> Rosemarie of TheBusyBudgeter.com
> Tai and Taalat of HisandHerMoney.com
> A.J. of PrinciplesofIncrease.com
> Michelle of ShopMyClosetProject.com
> Elle of CouplesMoneyPodcast.com
> Kristia of FamilyBalanceSheet.com
> For believing in me, encouraging me, and challenging me to come out of my comfort zone.

Cat Queen, a fabulous editor who became a friend in the process.

Lindsey Bagheri, for always believing in me, my mission, and for being my biggest cheerleader.

There have been many other amazing people to help me launch this book project, too many to possibly mention, but I truly thank you from the bottom of my heart.

Last, but certainly never least, I thank you my Heavenly Father, because without you, none of this would ever be possible.

RESOURCES

Use these resources to help you further along in your *Real Life on a Budget* journey!

Financially Fearless by Alexa von Tobel

The Total Money Makeover by Dave Ramsey

How to Budget for Irregular Income found on my site here: http://thebudgetmama.com/2014/08/budget-irregular-income.html

The One-Page Financial Plan by Carl Richards

Slaying the Debt Dragon by Cherie Lowe

Money Matters by Dave Ramsey

Debt-Free Workbook found on my site (in Excel) here: http://thebudgetmama.com/2015/03/4-steps-to-become-debt-free.html

Debt-Free in 24 Hours by Aja McClanahan

Become a Frugalista - Money-Saving Secrets for the Frugal Family Manager by Susan Heid

Dave Ramsey's Complete Guide to Money: The Handbook of Financial Peace University by Dave Ramsey

Six Dollar Family: From Six Dollars to Six Figures by Stacy Barr

Living Well, Spending Less: 12 Secrets of the Good Life by Ruth Soukup

The Great Debt Dump by Toni Husbands

Made in the USA
San Bernardino, CA
03 January 2016